The Tempest

For Kids

by
Lois Burdett

FIREFLY BOOKS

A Firefly Book

Published by Firefly Books Ltd. 1999
Copyright © 1999 Lois Burdett

Library of Congress Cataloguing-in-Publication Data available.

Canadian Cataloguing in Publication Data

Burdett, Lois
    The tempest for kids

(Shakespeare can be fun)
ISBN-13: 978-1-55209-326-9 (pbk.)
ISBN-10: 1-55209-326-3 (pbk.)

1. Children's plays, Canadian (English).* 2. Children's poetry, Canadian (English).* 3. Readers' theatre.
4. Shakespeare, William, 1564–1616 – Adaptations.
I. Shakespeare, William, 1564–1616. Tempest. II. Title.
III. Series.

PR2878.T4B87 1999 jC812'.54 C98-932685-3

Published in Canada by
Firefly Books Ltd.
66 Leek Crescent
Richmond Hill, Ontario
L4B 1H1

Published in the United States by
Firefly Books (U.S.) Inc.
P.O. Box 1338, Ellicott Station
Buffalo, New York 14205

Third Printing, 2009

Manufactured by Friesens in Altona, Manitoba, Canada in September, 2009, Job #50407

Design concept by Lois Burdett

Design production by
Fortunato Design Inc.

The Publisher acknowledges the financial support of the Government of Canada through the Book Publishing Industry Development Program for our publishing activities.

Other books in the series:
A Child's Portrait of Shakespeare
Twelfth Night for Kids
Macbeth for Kids
A Midsummer Night's Dream for Kids
Romeo and Juliet for Kids

Robin Wilhelm, The Beacon Herald

Lois Burdett's Grade 2 students

Foreword

"Give me the children until they are seven," said the Jesuit St. Francis Xavier, "and anyone may have them afterwards." Early influences are crucial in the formation of the faiths, tastes, and assumptions that characterize us throughout our adult lives, and the sooner an enthusiasm is embraced, the more likely it is to last a lifetime.

The same, unfortunately, is true of an aversion. How often have we heard adults proclaim Shakespeare to be too deep or difficult for them; and how often has their sense of inadequacy and exclusion been fostered in childhood by the dogged reverence of well-meaning but uninspired school teachers? "This is Great Literature, and it's good for you," goes the schoolroom mantra, and thus is perpetuated the idea of Shakespeare as medicine to be swallowed stoically rather than a giddy pleasure to be pursued at every opportunity.

Thank heaven for Lois Burdett, for teaching her students that great plays are great playthings, and that making theatre is a marvellous game, to be played with all your might.

Together, Lois and her students reinvent Shakespeare's plays, creating their own unique versions of his stories and his characters. They do, in essence, what Shakespeare did with his sources, and what all actors and directors do when they interpret a text for the stage. The process teaches presentational skills that will prove valuable in later life, but more importantly it teaches the vital truth that theatre is a living, collaborative, interpretive art. For Shakespeare's plays are not like rare and fragile artifacts in a museum: they were meant to be played with, and when placed in the hands of eager children they can reveal facets that we adults had overlooked, or forgotten.

The Tempest, for instance, is a profound and complex poem, rich in symbolism and allegory, a masterpiece of literary sophistication. But, as Lois's adaptation reminds us, it is also a fairy tale, complete with a monster, a maiden, a magician, an enchanted isle, a wicked brother, and a noble gesture of forgiveness. And those, finally, are the things that work on us, children and adults alike, in the theatre.

Tyrone Guthrie, the first Artistic Director of the Stratford Festival, remarked in a speech once, "The only great theatre you see is when you are young." Our imaginations are at their most open, their most accepting, when we are children, and we respond to theatrical characters and situations with an intensity that we can only yearn for as adults. When one succeeds in firing the imagination of a child, nothing can quench that enthusiasm – and when one fails, nothing can ignite it. To the child to whom he is introduced as a Very Important Man, indeed, Shakespeare may well remain a distant and impenetrable stranger. To the child fortunate enough to be introduced to him by Lois Burdett, he has every chance of being a friend and playmate for life.

Richard Monette

RICHARD MONETTE
Artistic Director
Stratford Festival

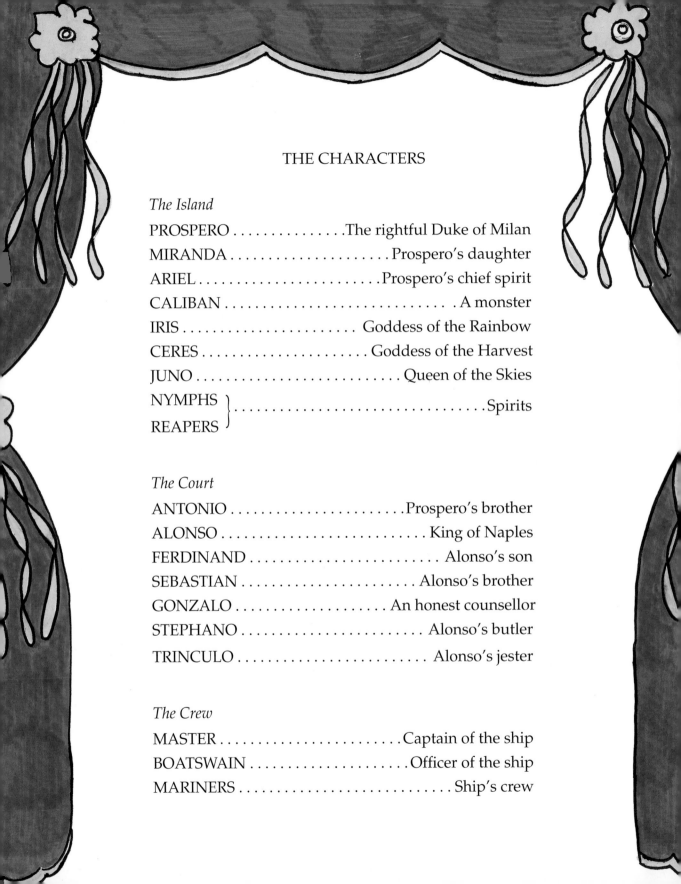

THE CHARACTERS

The Island

PROSPERO . . . . .The rightful Duke of Milan

MIRANDA . . . . Prospero's daughter

ARIEL . . . . .Prospero's chief spirit

CALIBAN . . . . A monster

IRIS . . . . Goddess of the Rainbow

CERES . . . . Goddess of the Harvest

JUNO . . . . Queen of the Skies

NYMPHS ⎫
. . . . Spirits
REAPERS ⎭

The Court

ANTONIO . . . . .Prospero's brother

ALONSO . . . . King of Naples

FERDINAND . . . . Alonso's son

SEBASTIAN . . . . Alonso's brother

GONZALO . . . . An honest counsellor

STEPHANO . . . . Alonso's butler

TRINCULO . . . . Alonso's jester

The Crew

MASTER . . . . .Captain of the ship

BOATSWAIN . . . . .Officer of the ship

MARINERS . . . . Ship's crew

Elly Vousden (age 8)

As I sit at my desk, my pen beckons me,
Words swirl in my mind and ache to be free.
A tale of magic begins to take seed,
With a raging storm, a tempest indeed.
More than thirty plays, I've written in the past.
So enjoy, my good friends. This is one of my last.

I convey you to Europe, off Italy's coast,
A sorcerer, Prospero, will soon be your host.
As we wait his arrival, cast down your eyes,
The ship below us is near its demise.
It tosses and heaves in the frenzied sea,
The storm boils with anger, wild as can be.
The wind howls in fury. Flames smother the ship.
Sails twist and tangle in the tempest's grip.
"Speak to the mariners," the captain implored.
"Take in the topsail!" the boatswain roared.

Katie Besworth (age 8)

Then Alonso, King of Naples, came along.
He hurried to see what had gone wrong.
He bellowed to the sailors, "Do something!
Must I remind you that I am the King?"
The boatswain shouted without a second thought,
"Waves care not for kings. Trouble us not!"
Ferdinand, the Prince, was also in dismay,
As he stumbled on deck in disarray.
He and Sebastian, the King's younger brother,
Trembled and clung to one another.
Antonio, Duke of Milan and Gonzalo, a lord,
Feared they'd be washed overboard.

Elly Vousden (age 8)

The mariners cried as they tilted and tossed,
"All lost! To prayers, to prayers! All lost!
Mercy on us! Our lives we submit.
Farewell! We split, we split, we split!"
The rigging trembled, the main sail ripped,
The rudder broke, the crow's-nest tipped.
With an ear-splitting crack the mast fell down.
Within minutes, it seemed, every soul would drown.
Beneath the dark waves the doomed boat sank.
Two figures watched from the rocky bank.
'Twas Prospero, the enchanter in control of this scene,
And his daughter, Miranda, a girl of fifteen.

The wind howled like it never had before. The sea moaned and groaned churning the waves into great sea dragons. It was like a roller coaster. Sounds of terrified people echoed through the flaming deck rising and falling with mournful cries. Then suddenly the ship cracked in two.

Story: Laura Bates (age 8)
Picture: Sophie Jones (age 9)

Miranda wailed in complete despair,
"They've all vanished in the storm out there.
My dearest father, your magic I deplore,
If you have caused this terrible uproar.
A brave vessel dashed all to pieces by your art,
Oh, the cry did knock against my very heart!
Pour souls, they perished!" Miranda sighed.
"Collect yourself!" Prospero replied.
"I have done nothing but in care of thee,
Lend thy hand and pluck my magic garment from me."

Oh dear father, stop it! Those poor people on that beautiful boat will perish! It grieves my heart to hear their pitiful cries, ringing in my ears. I never thought you were one to torment innocent people so. Well I see I am wrong. Their lives are being sucked from their cold, wet bodies.

Miranda

Story: Anika Johnson (age 8)
Picture: Megan Vandersleen (age 10)

9

Callyn Vandersleen (age 10)

"The time," said Prospero, "has come at last
To tell you the story of your past."
For the sorcerer, harsh images began to flow,
"Do you remember what happened twelve years ago?"
"'Tis far off," sighed Miranda, "like a dream you see.
Had I several women attending me?"
"You had, and more. Every need was provided,
Thy father was the Duke of Milan!" he confided.
"A prince of power!" Prospero's face grew intense.
"Sir, are not you my father?" Miranda cried in suspense.
Prospero cautioned his daughter, "Open thine ear,
Obey and be attentive, and you shall hear.
I was Milan's Duke, and ruled with care.
You were a princess and my only heir."

10

"Dear father! I don't understand what you say.
Why did we leave? Was there foul play?"
Prospero stared angrily out to sea,
"My brother, Antonio, detested me.
Ambition had turned his affection sour,
He desired my position and ultimate power.
To be in charge was never my great need,
My only wish was to sit and read.
I trusted him with affairs of state,
But he would send us to a watery fate."

My books were my life. I would sit at my desk, hour after hour drinking in all their secrets. The yellow pages aged with time were filled with wonders of the past. I loved my books even more than I loved being the Duke of Milan.

Prospero

Morgan Pel (age 8)

Elly Vousden (age 8)

11

Prospero paused, "Are you listening to me?"
Miranda replied, "Sir, most heedfully."
Her father continued, "Your uncle was cruel.
He thought I was an incompetent fool.
With Alonso, King of Naples, he shared this thought,
And together they hatched a terrible plot.
Oh, that a brother could be so vile,
Pretending he loved me all the while.
Alonso was also an enemy to me,
And he quickly agreed to my brother's plea."

Prospero

Calm yourself, my dear. There is reason for my magic. You see my brother did not understand my care and love for books. They were like friends to me. But Antonio was no friend. He thought only of himself. This was so long ago yet the ache in my heart rages on.
Prospero

Story: Kelsey Cunningham (age 8)
Picture: Ashley Kropf (age 10)

12

Prospero took a deep breath, as if in pain,
Then in a low voice, he spoke once again.
"That fateful evening I retired to bed,
With nothing but peaceful thoughts in my head.
I was unprepared for their jealousy and hate,
As my evil brother unlocked Milan's gate.
An army from Naples arrived that night.
Under cover of darkness they stole into sight.
The soldiers forced their way into my room,
And I awoke to confront my doom."

Dear Diary,
I was sleeping peacefully,
lost in a misty dream,
when suddenly an icy hand
gripped my shoulder! There
stood fifteen armed guards.
My whole body shuddered.
My heart pumped wildly
and my bones quivered
in fear. I struggled to free
myself. But it was hopeless!
    A petrified Prospero

Story: Brock Wreford (age 8)
Picture: Kimberly Brown (age 11)

13

"Why didn't these soldiers my uncle hired,
Destroy us at once?" Miranda inquired.
Prospero replied, "They dared not, you see,
My people had too much love for me.
We were pulled from our beds and smuggled to a boat,
A rotten carcass, that could hardly float.
Into my arms they forced you, my daughter,
Then pushed the boat into the water.
Oh dear Miranda, you were no more than three
When they thrust us upon the cruel sea.
With no sail or mast, we were left to die,
Even the rats deserted," he said with a sigh.

Anika Johnson (age 8)

"But the noble Gonzalo took pity on our plight,
And stocked our boat with food for that night.
Fresh water and rich garments, too, I recall,
And my books of magic, which I valued most of all.
Waves drove our little boat from shore,
And soon the land was seen no more."
Miranda cried, "What trouble was I then to you!"
Prospero answered, "You pulled me through.
My little cherub, your smile was my hope.
You gave me the strength I needed to cope."

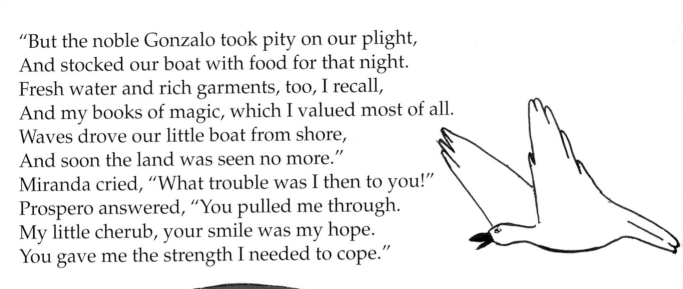

*Shannon Campbell
(age 10)*

Prospero arose, "Sit still, and hear,
The last of our sea-sorrow, then all will be clear.
Perhaps it was fate that kept us alive,
Or maybe it was the will to survive!
Whatever it was when our boat ran aground,
The paradise we saw held us spellbound.
For twelve years we've lived here by the sea,
With no other human company.
And on this deserted island serene,
Have I thy loving schoolmaster been."
"Thank you, Father, but please explain,
Why you raised this hurricane."

Elly Vousden (age 8)

Prospero replied, "By accident most strange,
Today, our future I'll rearrange.
My brother Antonio, and the King of Naples too,
Were returning to Milan with their royal crew.
Their boat was surrounded by my sea-storm,
And to my will they shall conform.
But ask no more questions. Thou art inclined to sleep."
And he charmed his daughter into slumber deep.
Then he raised his arms, "Come servant, come."
And from afar came an answering hum.

Dear Father,
I have learned many things from you, and indeed more than I would in Milan, from survival to what kinds of fruit to eat. I am so lucky to have a father like you. Your heart is as pure as glass and your soul is as gentle as a lamb.
                    Miranda

Story: Brock Wreford (age 8)
Picture: Mackenzie Donaldson (age 8)

Miranda

17

With a flash of wings and a shimmer of light,
Ariel, his attendant, flew into sight.
"Has your task been concluded?" Prospero inquired.
"Did you follow my instructions? What has transpired?"
Ariel was eager to report on the trip,
"I did all you asked: I boarded the King's ship,
And set it afire, as was your design.
All but mariners plunged in the foaming brine.
Ferdinand, the King's son, was the first to leap
Into the waves below, the swirling water deep."
Prospero looked pleased, "Was this near to shore?
And are they all safe? Quickly, tell me more!"

Anika Johnson (age 8)

18

Ariel continued with a contented sigh,
"Not a hair perished. Even their garments are dry.
They're now on our island, to different parts spread,
In small groups they wander, believing the others dead.
The King's son is alone and his mind is distraught,
He sits on the ground, his heart overwrought.
Their ship's at anchor in yonder cove deep,
And beneath the hatches the sailors sleep."
Prospero was delighted, "Now, let's review,
The next few hours and the work we must do."
"But you promised my freedom!" Ariel started to boil,
"And now, you tell me there's to be more toil."

Oh my master, I have done all the work and my wings are about to fall off. I zipped, zapped, zanged all over the ship. I made waves thirty metres tall and people were jumping like rats. So all's well that ends well. Now please give me my freedom!
Ariel

Ariel

Story: Mackenzie Donaldson (age 8)
Picture: Ashley Kropf (age 10)

Prospero turned on Ariel, with a threatening stare,
"Have you forgotten the Sycorax affair?
That foul witch, bent over with age,
Once ruled this island, in a towering rage.
You were her servant and obeyed her demands,
Forced to perform her abhorrent commands.
But when to her orders, you would not agree,
She used her power and trapped you in a tree.
Twelve years you suffered, and in that time she died,
Leaving you desperate and trapped inside.

Sycorax

Dear Prospero,
I do remember Sycorax and
I thank you loo times
over for letting me out of
that tree. It felt so gooey
and icky in there. The sap
kept dripping in my eyes and
the roots kept tripping me.
When you let me out I was
dancing with joy!
　　　　　　Ariel

Story: Kate Landreth (age 8)
Picture: Anika Johnson (age 8)

20

"Now Sycorax had borne a son, more ugly beast than man,
This wretched runt, a witch's brat, she christened Caliban.
Until we landed on this isle, there was no human soul,
And Caliban was ruler. He was in control.
I heard you groaning in the tree and made its trunk gape,
It was my kindly power that allowed you to escape."
Ariel was humbled, "I thank thee for your stand.
I promise, noble master, I'll do what you command!"
Prospero relented, "In two days, I'll set you free,
For now, be a sea nymph, invisible except to me."

Elly Vousden (age 8)

21

Taking these words as an exit cue,
The nimble sprite, Ariel, disappeared from view.
Prospero woke his daughter with a gentle shake,
"Dear heart, awake! Thou hast slept well. Awake!"
Then he stood and pointed to a nearby cave.
"Come on. We'll visit Caliban, my slave."
Miranda shuddered, "I don't wish to go near."
Caliban frightened her, and she cowered in fear.
Prospero reminded, "But he does make our fire,
Fetch in our wood, and serve as we require."
He called to Caliban, "Come forth, I say!
Come, thou tortoise! I have jobs for you today."
"There's wood enough within," Caliban growled.
"Thou poisonous toad!" the sorcerer scowled.

Prospero

Caliban, come you wretched creature. Don't raise thy temper at me. There is more work to be done. I rule this island and treat thee well. So don't get me angry. You should know by now that my wish is your demand!

Prospero

Story: David Marklevitz (age 8)
Picture: Matt Charbonneau (age 10)

Finally, the monster appeared to relent,
And from the den he stumbled, grotesque and bent.
"May a wind blister you all over," Caliban cursed,
"This island's mine! I was here first!
When you arrived, you made much of me,
Gave me water spiced with berries. Then I loved thee.
You taught me language, but would soon prove untrue,
All the charms of Sycorax, light on you!"
"Thou art a liar!" Prospero was riled.
"I treated you well, till you hurt my child.
I'll rack thee with cramps, till beasts run from thy din."
Caliban cringed, "I must obey. Prospero, you win!"

You villainous master!
I used to care for you
and in return this is
what I get...work work
work! I was lord of
this island until you
showed up. I know you
have great powers
but that gives you no
right to pick on me.
                    Caliban

Story: Rebecca Courtney (age 8)
Picture: Caitlin Ellison (age 8)

23

Meanwhile, Ariel continued to explore,
And found Ferdinand, who'd been washed ashore.
The Prince was in mourning for his father, the King,
When the spirit hovered near and began to sing.
"Come unto these yellow sands," was the sweet-toned plea.
"And then take hands," continued the haunting melody.
Ferdinand followed, but not of his own accord.
The mellow resonance could not be ignored.
Enchanted by its power, the Prince lost control,
"Where does this tune come from?" He couldn't see a soul.
"The song calms the torment that I felt before.
Wait, 'tis gone! The music sounds no more."
But soon the air quivered with a new refrain.
The mood was different when the spirit sang again.

Sydney Truelove (age 8)

"Full fathom five, thy father lies;
Those are pearls that were his eyes,
Sea nymphs hourly ring his knell,
Hark! Now I hear them, ding-dong, bell."
"What do these words mean?" Ferdinand thought.
His eyes filled with tears and his face felt hot.
"The ditty does remember my drowned father," he cried.
"This is no mortal business! My father must have died!"
Ferdinand was fraught with hopeless dismay,
He followed the sad music, as Ariel led the way.

Ariel

Many miles under the sea
Lying on the sand
Among the weeds that wave so free
Lies a lifeless man.

He is the King, your father
Mostly known as "sire"
Or "Your Majesty" rather
Whom most folks did admire.

He lies there, a poor old dead man
Coral are his bones
His royal ears no longer can
Hear the low sea moans.

His eyes are huge white pearls
Shiny as can be
Who could know he's talked with earls
For he lies here dead in the sea.

Poem: Anika Johnson (age 8)
Picture: Shannon Campbell (age 10)

25

Prospero was ready and knew just what to do,
When a short time later, Ferdinand stumbled into view.
He awoke Miranda, "Come, gaze and ponder!
Tell me, my daughter, what is that yonder?"
Miranda gasped in delight, "Oh, who can it be?"
She was in awe, "Is it a spirit that I see?"
"It eats and sleeps like us," Prospero replied.
"This man is from the wreck, and searches far and wide.
He's lost all his comrades, and his grief is acute.
He hopes to find them here, and wanders in pursuit."
Miranda was entranced, "That gentleman looks fine.
Oh Father, I might call him a thing divine!
For nothing natural I ever saw so noble."
She continued to stare, completely immobile.

Miranda

Oh dear father, what is this thing I see? It must be a spirit and a beautiful one too. Can we keep it? Can we, father? My heart pumps with excitement and my mind is exploding with love! This is my lucky day!
Miranda

Story: Mackenzie Donaldson (age 8)
Picture: Eliza Johnson (age 8)

Then, the Prince let out a heart-wrenching sigh.
As he raised his head, she quickly caught his eye.
Ferdinand was startled, overwhelmed with new cheer.
"Oh, beautiful goddess!" his voice was loud and clear.
He was drawn towards her, at a rapid pace.
And soon the two were standing, face to face.
"Do you dwell on this island?" his eyes were aglow.
"Oh you wonder!" he exclaimed, "Are you maid, or no?"
Miranda blushed, but was not afraid.
"No wonder, sir, but certainly a maid!"
"She speaks my language!" he joyfully cried,
"And all my sorrows to her I'll confide."
He told of the shipwreck and the sights he'd seen,
"When I'm King of Naples, I'll make you my Queen."

Ferdinand

In heaven's name is this an angel standing before me? I set my eyes on a new world! She is mortal like I! Oh joy! Oh fabulous rapture! Thrills and excitement are heading my way!
                    Ferdinand

Story: Elly Vousden (age 8)
Picture: Eliza Johnson (age 8)

Prospero listened, for he was close at hand,
Everything was working exactly as he'd planned.
But did Ferdinand truly love his daughter best?
Prospero decided to put him to a test.
The sorcerer spoke roughly, and looked him in the eye,
"You're here to steal my island. You are a spy!"
Ferdinand replied, "My thoughts you misconstrue.
No, I promise. Your words are untrue."
Poor Miranda pleaded, but to no avail.
Prospero continued to rant and rail,
"Speak not for him, Miranda. He is a traitor,
And I'll tell you lad what will happen later.
Old roots you shall eat. Seawater you will drink.
I'll manacle your feet, with pieces of chain link."

Prospero

Come Miranda, he is nothing
but a back-stabbing spy,
nothing but a spy. Miranda
don't be a fool. There are
dozens more men as
good as he. Pity him
no more.

Prospero

Story: David Marklevitz (age 8)
Picture: Katie Hopkins (age 7)

"I will resist!" cried Ferdinand, prepared to fight.
"Until your power overcomes my might."
Prospero waved his hands and fixed him to the ground.
Ferdinand was frozen and could not make a sound.
Miranda begged her father, "Do not be so stern!
He's gentle, and handsome. Show him some concern."
"Silence, Miranda! Not another word from you!"
The test was going well, and the spell he would undo.
When Ferdinand could move again, his legs were weak,
His fingers numb, and he could barely speak,
"Your threats do not scare me. Your wishes I'll obey,
If I can behold this maid, even once a day."

Anika Johnson (age 8)

29

"It works!" thought Prospero, as he withdrew.
He smiled to himself, and glanced back at the two.
For the happy pair, it was love at first sight.
Prospero was delighted and called to his sprite,
"Thou hast done well, fine Ariel, and I would be remiss
If I forgot to thank you. I'll free thee for all this.
In a short time, you may leave my command,
If you can accomplish my every demand."
"To the syllable!" Ariel grinned with glee.
Prospero turned to Ferdinand, "Come, follow me!"

Ariel

Dear Ariel,
I will set you free for this. I could not have done better myself. Now to put the final touches on my plan... They are two romantic lovers. But I will show Ferdinand that great prizes are not won easily.
Prospero

Story: Laura Bates (age 8)
Picture: Megan Vandersleen (age 10)

Meanwhile, on the island, in a different place,
King Alonso sat with a very long face.
He was with his nobles from the royal court.
Prospero's friend, Gonzalo, was lending his support.
"Beseech you, sir, be merry! Do not cry.
Our garments drenched in the sea are fresh and dry."
King Alonso moaned, "My gloom cannot be shed."
"He receives comfort like cold porridge!" Sebastian said.
Then the evil Antonio began to mock and jeer,
As Gonzalo continued to spread his cheer.

Oh my son, my only son
is dead, dead as a rock
without an owner!! I
despair to think about
him. He was my jewel.
My heart is choked
with the loss!
                    Alonso

King Alonso

Story: Ellen Stuart (age 8)
Picture: Sydney Truelove (age 8)

31

Prospero heard their taunts, aimed at his old friend,
And commanded Ariel to put it to an end.
The spirit played lullabies to encourage sleep.
Gonzalo felt drowsy, and curled in a heap.
King Alonso, too, quickly lost his zest.
His eyes began to droop, and he lay down to rest.
Ariel was watching, for all was at stake.
Sebastian and Antonio had been left awake.
They talked in low whispers, their thoughts ice cold.
Another evil plan was beginning to unfold.

It is hopeless! I have searched under bushes, up trees, and in creeks. My legs feel like mush and my bones are crumpled. Yet I still have not found my precious Ferdinand. I am truly broken. I never even said goodbye!

Alonso

Story: Emily Dunbar (age 8)
Picture: Ashley Kropf (age 10)

Alonso

Antonio inquired, "Since the Prince has drowned,
I wonder who'll be the next person crowned?
Noble Sebastian, indeed, you could be King!
You are his brother. Have you thought of such a thing?
My strong imagination sees a crown upon thy head.
Naples could be yours, if Alonso were struck dead."
"That's what you did in Milan," Sebastian replied.
"You disposed of your brother. He probably died."
Antonio nodded, "You're starting to see,
And look how well my garments sit upon me!"
Sebastian conceded, "Your example, I will follow.
You kill Alonso. I will kill Gonzalo."

Sebastian

Ashley Kropf (age 10)

Ariel was ready, hovering quite near.
"My master, through his art, foresees the danger here.
I'll warn Gonzalo, who'll see their swords held high."
"Preserve the King!" Gonzalo woke with a startled cry.
Alonso's eyes flew open, and he asked, "What's going on?
Explain your ghastly faces, and why your swords are drawn."
"We heard a roar like bulls, or rather lions!" Sebastian lied.
"We were trying to protect you!" Antonio quickly cried.
Gonzalo was troubled, "This is a strange case.
'Tis best we stand upon our guard or that we quit this place."
"Lead away," Alonso shouted, "We must find my son!"
Ariel flew off, "My lord shall know what I have done."

Sydney Truelove (age 8)

In another part of the island and close to shore,
Caliban was at work, carrying wood once more.
He was angry with his master, for the years of pain.
And the sorcerer's many spirits, he held in much disdain.
They had crushed him with cramps, and made his skin crawl,
Then pitched him in the mud. "I despise them one and all!
Oh no, here comes another, with more misery to bestow.
Prospero must be upset. I'm fetching wood too slow.
I'll fall flat so it won't see me!" Caliban cried in dread.
Then he dropped to the ground, his cloak over his head.
As he lay under the robe, there was the sound of bells.
He heard the spirit groan, "Phew, it smells!"

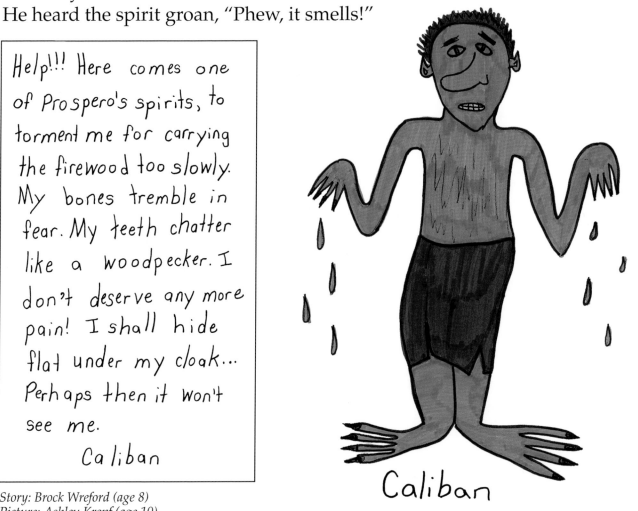

Help!!! Here comes one of Prospero's spirits, to torment me for carrying the firewood too slowly. My bones tremble in fear. My teeth chatter like a woodpecker. I don't deserve any more pain! I shall hide flat under my cloak... Perhaps then it won't see me.

Caliban

Caliban

Story: Brock Wreford (age 8)
Picture: Ashley Kropf (age 10)

But this was not a spirit, who approached so near.
His name was Trinculo, a jester by career.
He worked for King Alonso and was on that fated ship,
When it split apart, caught in the tempest's grip.
"What have we here?" The jester held his nose,
"Is it a man or fish, lying in repose?"
A very ancient stench wafted through the air.
"Is it dead or alive? This smell's beyond compare!
A fish!" he decided, and moved closer to inspect,
Then he saw its legs. His theory was incorrect.
"It's warm!" he cried, as he felt the lump in wonder,
Then jerked back in dismay, at the sound of thunder.
He crawled under the cape to escape the raging bellows,
"Misery acquaints a man with strange bed-fellows."

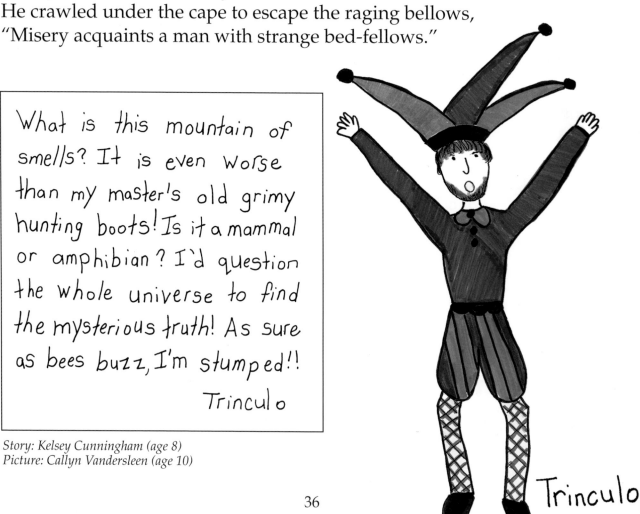

What is this mountain of smells? It is even worse than my master's old grimy hunting boots! Is it a mammal or amphibian? I'd question the whole universe to find the mysterious truth! As sure as bees buzz, I'm stumped!!

Trinculo

Story: Kelsey Cunningham (age 8)
Picture: Callyn Vandersleen (age 10)

Trinculo

36

The monster and the jester were shaking with fright,
When another from the ship stumbled into sight.
It was Stephano, the butler of the King.
He'd had too much to drink, and now began to sing,
"I shall no more to sea, to sea. Here shall I die ashore!"
Then he raised his bottle, and took a few swigs more.
Caliban moaned aloud, "Do not torment me, so!"
Stephano swaggered, "What sound is this, below?
A monster with four legs, and shaking in a fit?
It must have a fever. My wine will comfort it."
He lifted the cape, and poured wine down its throat.
Then he heard a voice at the other end of the coat.
"Four legs and two voices!" Stephano cried in shock,
"This is a devil and no monster! Now, two mouths talk!"

Eliza Johnson (age 8)

37

"I'll pour some in thy other mouth!" Stephano was quick.
"All my bottle's needed for a creature this sick!"
The jester recognized the voice, "Is that you, Stephano?
If it is, be not afeared, for I am Trinculo."
Stephano gasped in shock, "What is this about?"
But the legs did look familiar, so the butler pulled them out.
The men stared at each other, then frolicked in delight.
Stephano cried, "Stop! My stomach's not quite right!"
Caliban, too, arose, reeling from the wine.
He fell at Stephano's feet, "That liquid was divine!
Hast thou not dropped from heaven?" Caliban gaped in awe.
"Out of the moon," laughed Stephano, with a loud guffaw.
"I'll kiss thy foot!" vowed Caliban, "And never go astray.
I'll swear myself thy subject, and always will obey."

Eliza Johnson (age 8)

38

Caliban pranced about, with rejuvenated nerve,
"A plague upon Prospero, the tyrant whom I serve!
I'll bear him no more sticks, that I guarantee."
Then he pointed to Stephano, "I will follow thee!"
Caliban pursued him, singing of this plan,
"Caliban has a new master, get a new man!"
Trinculo was disgusted, "Stop this silly song.
To worship a drunk is foolish and wrong.
A most ridiculous monster!" he continued in dismay.
Stephano rejoiced, "Oh brave monster! Lead the way!"
The three linked arms, and tottered along the shore.
How could they know what the future held in store?

Stephano   Caliban   Trinculo

Anika Johnson (age 8)

39

Meanwhile, back at Prospero's abode,
Ferdinand was toting his heavy load.
Miranda implored, "Do not work so hard!
The orders of my father, you should disregard.
He's busy for three hours, so do what I suggest.
Put down those logs a while. You really need to rest!"
Ferdinand refused, "The sun will set before I'm done,
I cannot stop, dear mistress. My toil has just begun."
"Then let me help," she argued. "I'll haul them for a while."
"I would rather break my back," he answered with a smile.
"What is your name?" he asked. "I really need to know!"
"Miranda," she confided, "though I should not tell you so."

Dearest Ferdinand,
Oh stop that my love bud.
Put down those logs and
rest for a minute. You
are going to pull a
muscle for heaven's sake.
Oh Ferdinand, your smile
sends shivers down my
spine. I desperately want
you!

Miranda

Story: Courtney Vandersleen (age 8)
Picture: Erin Patterson (age 9)

40

"Admired Miranda! You are different from the rest.
So perfect and so peerless. Of all women, you're the best.
The instant that I saw you, it was like a tidal wave,
My heart flew to your service, and I became your slave."
"I am your wife," she promised, "if you will marry me."
Ferdinand fell upon his knees, "And I thus humble be."
Now all this while the lovers thought they were alone,
Little did they know they had a chaperon.
Prospero stood watching this tender scene unfold.
To him their love was precious as the finest, rarest gold.
"It is a joyous day! This union must be blessed."
His heart was satisfied, for they both had passed the test.

Shannon Campbell (age 10)

But trouble was brewing, back by the sea.
There was arguing among the gruesome three.
Stephano fancied he was the island's King.
To Caliban he was a god, and could do anything.
"How does thy honour? Let me lick thy shoe!"
Trinculo jeered, "Ignorant fool! You haven't got a clue."
The sneering and bickering went round and round.
So did the bottle. Soon all were half-drowned.
Then Ariel arrived, and added to the din.
Caliban was kneeling, his story to begin,
"I was cheated of my island. I did not have a choice."
"Thou liest!" whined Ariel, but in the jester's voice.

Stephano,
I will kiss thy feet, oh master. I will fetch thee firewood and dig nuts with my claws as sharp as bones. Oh hallelujah!!! I am saved. What would your first command be my lord? I will do anything for thee.
                    Caliban

Stephano

Story: Courtney Vandersleen (age 8)
Picture: Kate Vanstone (age 10)

Caliban turned on the jester, "I do not lie!"
"I said nothing!" chided Trinculo, "Your charge, I deny!"
"Quiet!" shouted Stephano, trying to keep the peace.
"Proceed, servant-monster. This argument must cease!"
Caliban continued, his words rushing faster,
"Stephano, to be lord, you must murder my old master!"
"Thou liest!" Ariel cried again, sounding like the jester,
Hoping their discord would grow and fester.
Trinculo threw up his hands, "I didn't say a word!
It must be the drink! Your thoughts are all blurred."
Just then a haunting tune echoed through the air.
But they were too confused to sort out this affair.
The music on the pipe and drum was low and hollow,
And the drunken trio felt they had no choice but follow.

Anika Johnson (age 8)

As this absurd scene on the shore transpired,
Back inland, the courtiers were tired.
Gonzalo groaned in agony, "I must take a break!
I can go no further, Sir. My old bones ache!"
King Alonso moaned, "I am weary, too!
My search is hopeless. Sleep is long overdue."
Antonio quickly pulled Sebastian to his side.
Their evil plans of murder must be clarified.
"Let it be tonight!" Antonio's voice was hard.
"They are so exhausted, they won't be on their guard."
"Tonight!" agreed Sebastian, but then their talk abated.
They heard solemn music, and felt strangely agitated.

Oh my old bones ache in grief. My legs can no longer carry my stiff body. Even worse we're on this deserted island without a speck of food. My skin is itching from all the mosquito bites. And who knows what creatures come out at night?
The tired Gonzalo

Gonzalo

Story: Sean McGarry (age 8)
Picture: Robyn Lafontaine (age 9)

The sombre sounds grew loud, and pervaded the air.
Suddenly, phantoms appeared out of nowhere.
They carried a table, laden with fruit and meat,
And beckoned the men to partake of the treat.
They circled and danced around the glorious food.
Then each bowed politely, to end the interlude.
As quickly as they came, they dissolved into the haze.
The nobles clung together, in a frightened daze.
King Alonso frowned, "We must not eat this meal!"
But the tantalizing smells held irresistible appeal.
The men moved quickly towards the banquet feast,
And with each step closer, their hunger increased.

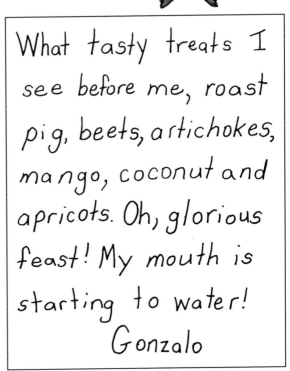

What tasty treats I see before me, roast pig, beets, artichokes, mango, coconut and apricots. Oh, glorious feast! My mouth is starting to water!
Gonzalo

Story: Elly Vousden (age 8)
Picture: Ashley Kropf (age 10)

45

The sky grew dark, the branches bowed low,
A furious wind began to blow.
A hideous bird swooped into sight,
And hovered above, like a parasite.
It was a huge beast, with blazing eyes.
All creatures shrank from its terrible cries.
Its razor sharp talons glistened in the air.
'Twas truly a monster, from a nightmare.

46

Shannon Campbell (age 10)

It pounced on the table with blood-curdling cries,
And all the food vanished before the men's eyes.
The King and his nobles were horrified,
As they huddled together, side by side.
The creature shrieked, "You are three men of sin,
Thinking only of yourselves and playing to win.
I have made you mad!" the great bird roared.
Fearing death, each man drew his sword.
But once again Prospero was in control,
Observing the scene from a nearby knoll.
His enemies had been caught by surprise.
The bird was really Ariel, in disguise.

"Remember," Ariel shrieked, "that you three
Exposed Prospero and his innocent child to the sea.
And for your foul deeds, you shall pay,
This will be your judgment day!"
Then the frightening bird vanished into the air,
As the spirits removed the table with flair.
King Alonso moaned, "My shame shall never ease.
Oh, what monstrous words are these!
The wind and the waves spoke of my crime,
I shall join my son, in the mud and the slime."
Prospero was contented, "They are in my power!"
My high charms work. The guilty cower!"

King Alonso

Guilt runs up and down my backbone. Prospero's name rings in my ears. Memories rush through my brain and the voice gets louder and louder. Shame chews at my soul and chokes my senses. My head grows dizzy and the image of Prospero I can never escape.
                                        Alonso

Story: Morgan Pel (age 8)
Picture: Sydney Truelove (age 8)

48

But now his thoughts turned to Miranda with cheer.
He was convinced Ferdinand's love was sincere.
The Prince was still toiling at the woodpile,
When Prospero approached him with a smile.
Ferdinand was startled by this look of goodwill.
And the old man's message gave him a thrill,
"Your wedding we will no longer postpone.
Here, before heaven, she is thine own."
Then he spoke to Ariel, "Summon my sprites.
We'll take an illusion to new magical heights."

Dear Ferdinand,
I am proud to announce that you passed the test. You lifted the logs like a pro. Your love runs pure and deep in each other's heart. I figured that out easily. Marry my daughter. You will have no complaint from me.
                    Prospero

Story: Rebecca Courtney (age 8)
Picture: Anika Johnson (age 8)

49

Within moments, Prospero's words proved true,
And shimmering spirits passed in review.
They each bowed low, as they danced along,
To honour the coming wedding in song.
The lovers were entranced by the wondrous show.
First, there was Iris, goddess of the rainbow.
Then Ceres, the messenger of harvest, drew nigh,
Followed by Juno, queen of the sky.
Still more spirits blessed the new romance.
Nymphs and reapers began a graceful dance.
But now, the scene changed on the wedding stage,
As Prospero arose in a furious rage.

Bronwen Summers (age 9)

50

He remembered Caliban and his murderous plot,
"They'll be here soon." Prospero was distraught.
When he saw his fury was causing duress,
He tried to calm the lovers' distress.
He beseeched the two, with arms extended,
"Be cheerful. Our revels now are ended.
These our actors, are melted into air,
And, like the baseless fabric of this vision rare,
The great globe itself shall one day be gone.
We are such stuff as dreams are made on,
And our little life is rounded with a sleep.
Bear with my weakness. Come, do not weep."

Love was in the air! Tears of joy trickled down my face at this romantic scene. Then evil thoughts gripped my mind with a BANG! The sky turned black in misery. Caliban's plan boiled in my brain. The game of life and death and magic itself will be played once again.
                    Prospero

Story: Willy Malmo (age 8)
Picture: Michelle Stevenson (age 11)

Prospero

Prospero summoned Ariel to his side,
"Where do the drunken fools abide?"
"My lord, through briers, I led them astray.
They're now mired in a filthy pond, not far away."
"Well done, my Ariel, release them if you please,
And hang royal garments on all these trees."
Both commands, Ariel quickly obeyed,
Then hid with Prospero to observe the charade.
They didn't wait long. In stumbled the three.
"Stephano," the jester cried, "a wardrobe for thee!"
Trinculo donned a cloak and added a crown.
Stephano grumbled, "I wanted that gown!"
"Thou fool, it is but trash!" Caliban cursed.
"Let it alone. And do the murder first!"

Laura Bates (age 8)

Suddenly, nearby, came horrible sounds,
The savage howling of hunting hounds.
They crashed out of the forest, lunging ahead.
The drunkards dropped the clothes, and hastily fled.
They roared in terror, as they raced through the fields,
With the wild dogs snarling at their heels.
Prospero, like a huntsman, urged the pack run faster.
This was his magic, for he was the master.
"Now does my project gather to a head,
My spells are working," Prospero said.
"Do this final service, Ariel, my friend,
And shortly, shall all my labours end."

Anika Johnson (age 8)

53

"How fares the King and lords?" Prospero inquired.
Ariel replied, "I did what you required.
They cannot move till you grant their release,
They suffer in silence and are not at peace.
Tears run down the good Gonzalo's face.
Though I am not human, I pity them, your Grace."
The spirit's tenderness touched Prospero's soul.
He knew it was time to release his control.
"My charms I'll break, their senses I'll restore,
And they shall be themselves, once more."

Elly Vousden (age 8)

He commanded his spirit, "Bring them to me.
Go now, Ariel. The truth they must see."
As his servant departed, duty bound,
Prospero drew a circle on the ground.
The men arrived, in a frenzied state,
And in the circle awaited their fate.
Paralyzed by the spell, they could not speak.
Prospero's power had now reached its peak.
"Ariel, fetch my crown, my robes, and my sword,
The Duke of Milan will soon be restored."
As he lifted the spell, the men gazed in dismay,
There stood the Duke they'd driven away.
The King wept in sorrow and fell to his knees,
"Thy dukedom, I resign. Oh, pardon me please!"

Sydney Truelove (age 8)

But Prospero was staring at Gonzalo, so kind.
"Sir, your honour cannot be defined.
Let me embrace you, a trusted friend so true."
Gonzalo was stunned, "Prospero, is it really you?"
Prospero took Antonio and Sebastian aside,
"I'm aware of your villainy, and that you both lied.
My brother, I forgive thy deeds so black.
But now I require my dukedom back."
Next, he turned to Alonso, the King,
"I know you believe you've lost everything.
Because you repent, I have a surprise.
Look into my cave and trust your eyes."

Dear Prospero,
I beg your forgiveness.
It is more important
than the most gleaming
sapphire. I was a fool
to set you off into
that unpredictable ocean.
From a shamed
Alonso

Story: Brock Wreford (age 8)
Picture: Ashley Kropf (age 10)

Alonso

56

King Alonso peered through the shadows inside.
Prospero's cave was indeed occupied!
There sat his son, alive and well.
Could this be true, or just another spell?
By Ferdinand's side was a girl playing chess.
Alonso felt joy he could not suppress,
"If this prove a vision, I'll pay the price,
One dear son, shall I lose twice!"
Ferdinand looked up, and his father he spied,
"Though the seas threaten, they are merciful," he cried.
"I have cursed them without cause. What's lost is found!"
Miranda was watching the scene spellbound.

Elly Vousden (age 8)

"Oh wonder! How many goodly creatures are there here!"
Miranda marvelled with delight, as she drew near.
"Brave new world that has such people in it," she cried.
The King asked his son, "Is this a goddess by your side?"
"Sir, she is mortal and for her, this man I owe."
He gestured to her father, "The famous Prospero.
This lady makes him my second father," he said.
"In Naples, Miranda and I plan to be wed."
Alonso approved, "And I gain a daughter fair.
Give me your hands. I will bless you both in prayer."

To my love Ferdinand,
Ferdinand I so much
want to get married.
When I first saw
you, you looked so
good! Your face was
such an amazing sight.
Your smile was beaming,
your hair was shining
and your eyes grabbed
mine. You know how
much I love you!
          Your sweetie pie
             Miranda

Story: Marissa Izma (age 8)
Picture: Robyn Lafontaine (age 9)

Amidst all this rejoicing, laughter, and fun,
There was still one deed that needed to be done.
Prospero told Ariel, "Set the drunkards free.
Untie the spell! Bring them forth to me."
Still in stolen clothes, they tumbled into view.
Their capes were torn and their hats askew.
"Are those my servants?" wondered the King.
He pointed to the monster, "Now, there's a strange thing!"
Caliban saw his master, and once again was awed,
"I was a fool to mistake a drunkard for a god."
Prospero agreed, "To earn pardon, you must behave."
Then he beckoned to the lords, "Come rest, in my cave.
In the morning, for Naples, we shall set sail,
And I promise you, only calm seas will prevail."

Caliban

Stephano

Trinculo

Lisa Hoeg (age 10)

59

Then for the last time, he called Ariel aside,
Prospero's eyes were filled with pride.
"My dainty sprite, you are a friend indeed,
And now I grant you, your only need.
With my magic power, I set you free,
But in my heart, you shall stay with me.
Come now, Ariel, please draw nigh,
The hour has arrived to say goodbye."

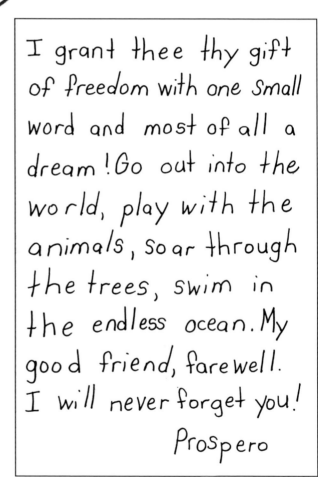

I grant thee thy gift of freedom with one small word and most of all a dream! Go out into the world, play with the animals, soar through the trees, swim in the endless ocean. My good friend, farewell. I will never forget you!
Prospero

Story: Laura Bates (age 8)
Picture: Ashley Kropf (age 10)

60

Ariel was filled with joy and despair,
He and his master had been such a pair.
"We have succeeded in every endeavour,
And, noble Sir, I shall miss you forever.
For my precious freedom, I will always bless you."
Then he bowed his head and quietly withdrew.
Prospero smiled, "In your happiness, I rejoice.
Now it's up to me, to make the final choice."

Oh Prospero, you have
been so faithful to me.
I cannot bear to leave
you. Rivers of tears
shower my face with
sadness. They cover my
hopes of being free
with a dark cloud of
mourning. Dear Prospero,
your love and care is in
my heart and will stay
with me forever.
                    Ariel

Story: Katie Besworth (age 8)
Picture: Ashley Kropf (age 10)

Prospero ascended the highest peak.
Shrouded in moonlight, he began to speak,
"This rough magic, I here abjure,
I'll break my staff. My promise to ensure."
Then he cast his treasured books into the sea,
And for the first time, he too was free.
His power and magic, he could not redeem,
He stood alone, a man with a dream.

"We are such stuff as dreams are made on," the fine fabric of a golden tale. The love bird carries joy to end this very day with cheers and merry merry sighs. The curtain closes. My words echo through, the earth's golden mist and rainbows of glory fall from the sky.

Story: Caitlin Ellison (age 8)
Picture: Robyn Lafontaine (age 10)

"Now my charms are all overthrown,
And what strength I have's mine own,
Which is most faint: now 'tis true,
I must be here confined by you.
As you from crimes would pardoned be,
Let your indulgence set me free."

Anika Johnson (age 9)

Parents and Educators

This book can be used for a variety of activities, either at home or in the classroom. Here are a few suggestions you might find helpful.

- Locate Milan and Naples on a map of Italy.

- Research famous shipwrecks from history.

- Make a three-dimensional map of the island, and add special features.

- Write newspaper accounts of Prospero's banishment from Milan and of the shipwreck.

- Share magic tricks and optical illusions.

- List all the incidents of magic in the play. Survey and tally for personal favourites, and graph the results.

- Create a tableau (a "frozen picture") of a particular scene.

- Debate Prospero's strengths and weaknesses as the Duke of Milan, a father, a magician, and the ruler of the island.

- Pick a character's name and write a description of the island from that character's point of view.

- Choreograph a dance for the nymphs and reapers in honour of Miranda and Ferdinand's forthcoming marriage.

- Conduct a press conference with Prospero, Antonio, and King Alonso, on their return to Milan.

Caitlin Ellison (age 8)

- Compose your own music for Ariel's songs.

- Create a tourism brochure advertising the island for a cruise.

- Draw a costume sketch of Prospero's magic cloak.

Educators who wish to stage performances of *The Tempest for Kids* should contact the author to request permission:
Fax: (519) 273-0712
E-mail: lburdett@shakespearecanbefun.com

Special thanks to Ann Stuart for her friendship, kind assistance, and interest in the book.

Front cover: Megan Vandersleen (age 10)
Title page: Anika Johnson (age 8)
Back cover picture: Elly Vousden (age 8)